Title: Freeing Your True Self: Breaking the Chains of Narcissistic Control

Subtitle: Reclaim Your Confidence, Set Boundaries, and Heal from Toxic Relationships for Good

Peter Pace

Copyright © [2024] by Peter Pace

Publisher: [Peter Pace] Printed in the United States of America

Acknowledgments

Writing this book has been a journey of healing, growth, and self-discovery, and it would not have been possible without the support, wisdom, and encouragement of so many people.

To my family and friends, thank you for your unconditional love and support throughout this process. You have been my anchors and my inspiration. Your faith in me has been the light that guided me, and I am forever grateful.

A heartfelt thank you to my mentors and colleagues in the fields of psychology and personal growth. Your insights and guidance have been invaluable. I am grateful for the countless conversations, shared wisdom, and expertise that shaped this book.

To my readers—those who are on the path to reclaiming their true selves—this book is for you. Your courage to confront difficult truths, to heal, and to grow is nothing short of inspiring. Thank you for entrusting me with a part of your journey. I hope these pages offer you comfort, empowerment, and strength.

Finally, thank you to everyone who has supported this project in ways big and small. Your kindness, belief, and dedication mean the world to me.

With gratitude Peter Pace

About the Author

Peter Pace is a passionate advocate for personal empowerment, healing, and self-discovery. With a deep understanding of the psychological impacts of toxic relationships, Peter dedicates his work to helping individuals break free from the constraints of narcissistic influence and reclaim their true selves.

Drawing from years of research, personal insights, and a commitment to mental well-being, Peter guides readers through a journey of understanding, resilience, and growth. His empathetic approach empowers others to set healthy boundaries, build confidence, and embrace a life rooted in self-compassion and authenticity.

In addition to his work as an author, Peter is a speaker and mentor, inspiring audiences to overcome adversity and lead lives defined by purpose and freedom. Through his writing, Peter continues his mission to uplift, empower, and transform lives, one chapter at a time.

Content

Introduction*

- **Understanding the Chains: Narcissism and Its Impact**
- **Why It's Not You: Breaking Free from Self-Blame**

In a world where connections are abundant but transitory, many people become enmeshed in relationships that leave them feeling confused, weary, and reduced. Among the most poisonous of these relationships are those with narcissists, who have an inflated sense of self-importance and a fundamental lack of empathy. These interactions can be extremely harmful, locking victims in cycles of emotional manipulation, self-doubt, and insecurity. This book, Freeing Your True Self: Breaking the Chains of Narcissistic Control, offers hope to individuals who want to grasp the nature of narcissism and regain their sense of self.

Understanding the Chains: Narcissism and its Impact.

Narcissism is a complicated psychological trait that occurs on a continuum, impacting not only the individual but also those around them. Narcissism is fundamentally defined by an inordinate desire for praise and a great disdain for the sentiments and needs of others. Narcissists thrive on control and frequently utilize tactics like gaslighting, manipulation, and emotional abuse to retain their power in relationships.

Narcissism can have far-reaching and long-term consequences for its victims. Many people question their reality, feel inadequate, and distrust their own senses. The initial charm and charisma of a narcissist can be alluring, creating the illusion of a perfect connection. However, as the relationship progresses, the veneer frequently breaks down, revealing a pattern of emotional upheaval that can leave one feeling imprisoned and powerless.

Victims in narcissistic relationships might experience a variety of psychological repercussions including anxiety, depression, and low self-esteem. These people frequently internalize the narcissist's negative messages, believing that they are somehow to blame for the harm they experience. This mindset promotes a cycle of self-blame and maintains narcissistic control over their life.

Understanding narcissism's mechanisms and consequences is the first step toward breaking away from its grip. Recognizing the indicators of narcissistic behavior is critical for identifying unhealthy relationships and protecting oneself from future harm. It is critical to recognize that you are not alone; many others have encountered comparable challenges and come out stronger on the other side.

Why It Isn't You: Breaking Free from Self-blame

One of the most prevalent and detrimental effects of being involved Internalization of blame is a characteristic of narcissistic individuals. Victims are frequently ensnared in a web of self-doubt, questioning their behaviors, emotions, and even their value. They may question themselves, "What did I do wrong?" or "Why can't I just make them happy?" This never-ending cycle of self-blame is a potent tactic of manipulation used by narcissists to maintain control over their victims.

It is critical to understand that the poison in a narcissistic relationship is not indicative of your worth or character. Narcissists thrive on making others feel inferior, keeping their victims reliant and servile. This relationship can cause an overpowering sense of shame and guilt, disguising the truth: a narcissist's behavior is rooted in their own insecurities and dysfunctions, not your activities or worth.

Breaking free from self-blame requires a fundamental adjustment in viewpoint. It demands you to accept that you are not responsible for the narcissist's actions or emotions. It is about releasing the guilt that has been wrongfully imposed on you and acknowledging that you deserve to be treated with respect and decency. The path to self-forgiveness and healing begins with the realization that you have the ability to reclaim your narrative.

In this book, we'll look at the intricacies of narcissistic behavior and its impact on relationships, as well as practical solutions for healing and reclaiming your true self. You will learn how to recognize narcissistic characteristics, set appropriate boundaries, and build a revitalized sense of self-esteem. Most Importantly, you will realize that your path to healing is about more than just survival; it is about thriving and accepting your true self.

Reclaiming Your Power: A Journey to Self-Rediscovery

Following a relationship with a narcissist, many people find themselves at a crossroads, dealing with feelings of bewilderment and loss. The emotional toll can be significant, frequently resulting in a strong sense of fragmentation. Without this individual, who am I? What do I really want? Am I capable of experiencing happiness again? These questions might seem overwhelming, but they also mark the start of a profound path of self-discovery and reclaiming personal authority.

Understanding Your True Self

At the center of this journey is a genuine desire to reconnect with your own self. The constant criticism, manipulation, and emotional abuse that characterizes narcissistic relationships can distort your self-perception, leaving you confused of your values, goals, and ambitions. The initial step toward Reclaiming your authority entails an introspective journey to find who you are outside of the narcissist's influence.

Begin by reflecting on your basic values—what is most important to you. Which activities provide you joy? Which dreams have you placed on hold? Self-exploration can help you filter through layers of uncertainty and confusion, revealing the essence of your existence. Journaling can be a valuable tool in this process since it allows you to express your thoughts and feelings without judgment. As you write, you may rediscover long-buried passions and desires, reigniting the flame of your own self.

Importance of Setting Boundaries

As you continue on this journey of self-discovery, it becomes increasingly important to set and maintain appropriate limits. Narcissistic Relationships frequently obscure the distinction between self and other, making it harder to identify one's own wants and desires. Setting boundaries is an act of self-respect and empowerment, indicating to yourself and others that you care about your well-being.

Begin simply by recognizing areas in your life where you feel overburdened or compromised. This could involve relationships, work obligations, or personal commitments. Learn to say no without feeling guilty, and put your mental and emotional well-being first. Setting boundaries will help you not only protect your newfound sense of self, but also develop healthier relationships with people who respect your limits.

cultivating self-compassion.

Cultivating self-compassion is an important step in regaining your power. After suffering the severe comments and emotional invalidation characteristic of a narcissistic relationship, it is normal to absorb negative thoughts about oneself. To break out from this pattern, practice self-kindness and acceptance.

Begin by acknowledging that healing is a nonlinear process with ups and downs, triumphs and setbacks. Treat yourself with the same compassion you would show a dear friend. When negative ideas occur, counter them with affirmations of your own worth and strength. Remember that you are not defined by your history or the actions of others; you are a multifaceted, worthy person with the ability to develop and heal.

Creating a supportive environment.

It is critical to surround oneself with supportive people while you journey through the process of self-discovery. Look for friends, relatives, or support groups that understand your struggle and can Provide encouragement. Sharing your experiences with individuals who sympathize can be extremely empowering and reaffirm your sense of self.

Consider joining networks focused on personal development, whether online or in person. These settings frequently create a sense of belonging, allowing you to share your story, learn from others, and receive crucial insights into your own recovery journey.

Embracing the Future of Possibilities

Reclaiming your power and rediscovering your true self entails more than just healing from past trauma; it also entails embracing a future full of possibilities. As you let go of narcissistic control, you will discover that the world opens up in ways you never anticipated. This increased independence enables you to explore your passions, establish meaningful relationships, and create a life that is true to yourself.

Visualize your perfect future—how does it look? What do you hope to achieve? Allow yourself to dream large and set achievable goals that reflect your values and desires. This vision will be your compass, guiding you as you travel the route ahead.

Part I: Recognizing Narcissistic Influence**

1. **Identifying the Narcissist in Your Life**

Recognize Narcissistic Influence

Navigating relationships with narcissists may be extremely difficult, frequently leaving people feeling confused, exhausted, and disorientated. The first step toward reclaiming your authority is to detect the signs of narcissistic influence. This section will assist you in identifying the narcissists in your life by exploring their characteristics and techniques, recognizing early warning signs of toxic behavior, and exposing the manipulative ways they use to maintain control.

Identifying a Narcissist in Your Life To understand how to negotiate relationships with narcissists, you must first get aware of the characteristics and strategies that are typically linked with narcissistic behavior. Narcissists frequently demonstrate a unique set of features that distinguish them from others.

Traits and Tactics: Understanding Narcissistic Patterns

Narcissistic individuals frequently exhibit a spectrum of Defining characteristics include:

Grandiosity: Narcissists have an overblown sense of self-importance. They frequently overstate their accomplishments, talents, and contributions, believing they are superior to others and deserve preferential treatment. This grandiosity might be expressed as bragging, boasting, or an insatiable desire for adoration.

Lack of Empathy: The inability or reluctance to sympathize with others is a defining feature of narcissism. Narcissists frequently disregard the sentiments and needs of those around them, resulting in callous behavior and emotional neglect. This lack of empathy might make it difficult to form meaningful relationships.

Entitlement: Narcissists typically believe that they are entitled to special privileges and exemptions from the rules that everyone else follows. This entitlement can result in the exploitation of others and the expectation that others will Provide for their necessities without expecting anything in return.

Manipulation: Narcissists are skillful manipulators who use techniques like gaslighting, guilt-tripping, and emotional blackmail to influence others around them. They frequently manipulate events to their benefit, leaving their victims questioning their views and reality.

Despite their apparent confidence, narcissists frequently have fragile self-esteem that relies largely on external validation. When their self-esteem is damaged, they may react defensively to criticism by expressing rage or aggression.

These characteristics are frequently interlaced, resulting in a complex web of behavior that can be difficult to navigate. Recognizing these patterns can help you detect narcissistic people in your life and take preventative measures to protect yourself.

Red Flags & Warning Signs: Detecting Toxic Behavior Early.

Detecting harmful behavior early can be Important for protecting your emotional well-being. Here are some common red signs that could signal the existence of a narcissist in your life.

Excessive Flattery: Although praises might be genuine, narcissists frequently employ excessive flattery to entice you and create a sense of duty. If someone's praise appears fake or overdone, it could be a symptom of manipulation.

Lack of Accountability: Narcissists rarely accept responsibility for their behavior. They frequently divert blame to others, refuse to admit their mistakes, and may even gaslight you into believing you are too responsible for their actions. If you're continually apologizing or defending yourself, that's a major red flag.

Controlling behavior: Narcissists frequently want to control their relationships by dictating how you should Feel, think, or act. They may criticize your choices, cut you apart from friends and family, or undercut your decisions. This domineering approach might create a toxic environment in which you feel increasingly powerless.

Inconsistent Behavior: Narcissists may alternate between idealization and devaluation, lavishing you with adoration one minute and insulting you the next. This contradiction might cause confusion and emotional distress, making you question your worth.

Entitlement to Your Time and Energy: Narcissistic entitlement occurs when someone constantly demands your attention and energy without reciprocation. This conduct might leave you feeling tired and exploited since they place their needs over yours.

Knowing these red signs can help you spot toxic conduct before it increases, allowing you to take the necessary Steps to keep oneself safe from further harm.

Unmasking Manipulation: How Narcissists Control and Deceive

Narcissists are skilled manipulators who keep control over their victims. Understanding their strategies is critical for breaking away from their control. Here are some frequent methods used by narcissists.

Gaslighting is a manipulative tactic that distorts reality to make you question your perceptions and sanity. A narcissist may reject facts, twist your comments, or even construct events to cause confusion and self-doubt. Over time, you may come to rely on the narcissist's version of reality rather than your own intuition.

Love Bombing: At the start of a relationship, narcissists frequently engage in "love bombing," showering their victim with affection, attention, and presents to develop an intense emotional bond. This overwhelming display of love can make it difficult to detect signals of their true character until you are fully committed in the relationship.

Triangulation: Narcissists frequently utilize triangulation to create splits and encourage jealousy, turning others against one another. They keep control over the story by involving a third party in conflicts or relationships, as well as manipulating the emotions of others.

Playing the Victim: Narcissists frequently use a victim mindset to get sympathy and escape accountability. They can avoid criticism by portraying themselves as the victimized party and manipulating others into feeling guilty for their suffering.

Silent Treatment: This approach involves withholding communication and emotional support as a means of punishment or management. The silent treatment might make you feel isolated Anxiety and a desire for validation allow the narcissist to reestablish control at your expense.

Recognizing these manipulative strategies is critical to reclaiming control and safeguarding your mental well-being. As you learn to recognize and understand the narcissists in your life, you can take proactive efforts to regain your autonomy and set better boundaries.

2. **Breaking the Spell: The Allure and Danger of Charisma**

- Why Narcissists Are So Magnetic

- The Cycle of Idealization and Devaluation

Breaking the Spell: The Allure and Risks of Charisma

Narcissists have a distinct charisma that may attract individuals like moths to a flame. Their charismatic personalities frequently attract those around them, making it impossible to detect the underlying toxicity until it is too late. Understanding why narcissists are so appealing—and the hazards that accompany that allure—is critical for identifying their influence in your life.

Why Are Narcissists So Magnetic?

Narcissists emit a powerful charisma. Several key elements contribute to this magnetism, including:

Confidence: Narcissists frequently exude an excessive amount of self-confidence, which can be appealing to others. This confidence can be misinterpreted as competence, making them appear like natural leaders or enticing partners. People are captivated by their aggressiveness, and frequently feel I was inspired by their energy.

Chand charisma: arm Narcissists are typically adept in social relations. They can be humorous, engaging, and enjoyable to be around, making people feel special and cherished in the present. This appeal can generate a false sense of intimacy, causing people to miss warning signs.

Fantasy and Idealization: During the early phases of a relationship, narcissists frequently idealize their target, lavish them with care and attention. This "love bombing" generates a fantasy-like experience that can be seductive, leading people to ignore any dangerous behaviors.

Excitement and Adventure: Narcissists frequently thrive on drama and excitement, which can instill a sense of adventure in relationships. Their impetuous attitude can make conversations feel thrilling, allowing others to feel alive in ways they might not have had previous experience.

While these characteristics can provide an initial charm, they frequently conceal a darker reality that emerges as the relationship unfolds.

Cycle of Idealization and Devaluation

One of the most pernicious elements of interactions with narcissists is the cycle of idealization and depreciation. Individuals who follow this pattern may experience emotional whiplash and profound confusion.

Idealization: In the beginning, narcissists frequently placed their relationships on a pedestal, showering them with praise and devotion. During this stage, you may feel as if you are living in a fairy tale, with the narcissist fulfilling all of your desires and making you feel cherished. This stage strengthens the link, forming an emotional reliance that makes it difficult to leave.

Devaluation: As time passes, the appeal starts to wane. Narcissists Typically, they move from idealization to devaluation, insulting, ridiculing, and undermining their partner's self-worth. This quick transition may leave you feeling puzzled and trying to reclaim the affection you once had. The discrepancy causes perplexity, prompting you to question your reality and value.

This repetitive cycle can make it difficult to move away from the connection. The high of idealization frequently keeps people locked in, wanting to reclaim the initial affection and approval they once felt. Understanding this cycle is vital for spotting narcissists' harmful influence and recovering control of your life.

3. **Gaslighting and Reality Distortion**

- How Narcissists Twist Truths to Control

- Becoming Gaslight-Resistant: Techniques to Stay Grounded

Gaslighting and Reality Distortion

Gaslighting is one of the most harmful strategies used by narcissists, causing victims to question their own reality and perceptions. Understanding how narcissists distort reality and understanding strategies to keep grounded are critical to breaking free from their grip.

How Narcissists Twist the Truth to Control

Gaslighting is a strategy used by narcissists to manipulate and keep control over their victims. Here are some of the ways they manipulate the truth:

Denying Reality: Narcissists frequently deny or distort facts, using phrases like "That never happened" or "You're just imagining things." This strategy undermines your trust in your memory and perspective, causing you to question your experiences. Over time, this might lead to a sense of separation from reality.

Blame shifting: When confronted with Narcissists usually shift blame onto their victim. For example, if they have wounded you, they may claim that you are overly sensitive or that you drove them to behave in a particular way. This manipulative behavior causes uncertainty and guilt, making you feel accountable for their actions.

Projection: Narcissists frequently project their vulnerabilities and flaws onto others. If they're dishonest, they might accuse you of lying or being untrustworthy. This strategy diverts attention away from their behavior and causes you to question your own integrity.

Selective Memory: Narcissists may conveniently "forget" discussions or occurrences that do not fit their narrative. This selective remembering can make you feel dissatisfied and invalidated since your point of view is ignored or diminished.

Creating Doubt: By questioning your view of Narcissists instill uncertainty in your thinking. You may ask yourself, "Did I really see that?" or "Am I overreacting?" This self-doubt might keep you stuck in the relationship, searching for clarification and approval.

These approaches have a very confusing and disorienting effect when taken together. Victims of gaslighting frequently feel as if they are walking on eggshells, continuously attempting to please the narcissist while losing their sense of self in the process.

Becoming Gaslight Resistant: Techniques to Stay Grounded

that build resilience against gaslighting, you must establish techniques that reaffirm your sense of reality and self-worth. Here are some helpful strategies to keep you grounded:

Document your experiences: Keep a journal of your emotions, talks, and experiences. Writing things down can Help to consolidate your recollections and bring clarity when doubts occur. If a narcissist tries to alter your reality, look to your notes for validation.

Trust your instincts: Pay attention to your feelings and gut reactions. If something feels off, it probably is. Learning to trust your intuition will help you avoid second-guessing yourself in the face of manipulation.

Seek external validation: Talk about your experiences with trusted friends or family members who can provide objective feedback. When a narcissist tries to distort your reality, sharing your opinions with others might assist clarify and validate it.

Set Boundaries: Make it plain what behavior you will and will not accept. If a narcissist violates these boundaries, strongly express yourself and reiterate Your boundaries. Maintaining your boundaries can help limit the narcissist's capacity to manipulate you.

Prioritize activities that boost your mental and emotional well. Self-care can boost your self-esteem and create a solid base upon which to resist exploitation. Mindfulness, exercise, and nature walks can all help you feel more grounded.

Educate Yourself: Understanding narcissism and gaslighting might help you spot the signs of manipulation. The more you understand these strategies, the more prepared you will be to negotiate relationships with narcissists.

Using these tactics, you can build a barrier against the negative impacts of gaslighting, allowing you to restore your reality and self-worth. Recognizing the methods of narcissists and remaining centered in your truth is critical. A step toward breaking free from their influence and living a happier, more true life.

Part II: Reclaiming Your Confidence**

4. **Building Inner Strength**

- Releasing Self-Doubt and Reclaiming Confidence

- How to Separate Your Self-Worth from Their Validation

Reclaiming Your Confidence

Building Inner Strength

Rebuilding your confidence and inner power is one of the most transforming aspects in recovering from narcissistic influence. Narcissistic relationships can deplete your sense of self, leaving behind self-doubt and a dependency on external affirmation. This chapter offers strategies for overcoming self-doubt and regaining confidence, allowing you to divorce your self-worth from the need for the narcissist's approval and recover a deep, unshakable confidence within.

Releasing Self-Doubt and Regaining Confidence Years of manipulation and control can cause significant self-doubt. When you're continuously second-guessing yourself or seeking approval from someone who enjoys throwing you off balance, it's easy to lose sight of your own power. Regaining confidence starts with eliminating the assumptions and doubts created by Narcissistic impact.

Challenge Negative Self-Talk: Many persons who have been through narcissistic relationships develop negative inner dialogues such as "I'm not good enough" or "I always mess things up." Recognize that these thoughts are often based on the narcissist's critiques and projections. Reframe these beliefs with affirming comments like, "I am capable," or "I am worthy of respect and kindness."

Identify and Celebrate Your Strengths: Reconnecting with your particular strengths is an important step toward regaining confidence. Reflect on past accomplishments, abilities, or attributes that make you proud. Celebrating these features might help you regain faith in yourself by reminding you of your strength and abilities.

Practice Self-Compassion: Developing compassion for oneself is critical to overcoming the narcissist's harsh self-judgments. Allow yourself Feel empathy and understanding for what you have been through. Treat yourself as you would a friend, with kindness instead of judgment. Self-compassion can foster internal growth and confidence.

create Small Goals and Celebrate Progress: Confidence builds with experience, so create attainable goals that will allow you to achieve achievement. Each minor triumph strengthens your strengths and helps you gain momentum. With each victory, your self-doubt fades, and you may move forward with a greater sense of confidence in yourself.

Self-doubt is released gradually. Over time, when you replace negative thoughts with positive affirmations and praise your abilities, you will become more grounded in a firm confidence that is difficult to shake.

How to Differentiate Your Self-Worth from Theirs Validation

When you are used to defining your worth based on a narcissist's approval, shifting your self-worth inward can feel strange and uncomfortable. However, true confidence and inner strength emerge when you stop relying on outward affirmation. Here are some techniques to help you regain control of your self-worth:

Reevaluate Your Values and Priorities: Take the time to consider what is genuinely important to you—your values, interests, and priorities. These are the roots of your identity, regardless of others' opinions. As you focus on living in accordance with your own principles, your need for external validation decreases, and your self-worth is based on your honesty.

Create Your Own Positive Feedback Loop: When you've been trained to seek validation, it can be tough to rely entirely on your own judgment. Begin by acknowledging and affirming your accomplishments, no matter how minor. Practice recognizing your own efforts and the traits you bring to situations. Positive self-reflection can be a source of fulfillment, boosting your self-esteem.

Stop Over-Apologizing: People who have been subjected to narcissistic influence frequently find themselves apologizing for their emotions or demands. Recognize that you do not need permission or approval to feel or be who you are. Stand solid in your worth and remind yourself that you deserve to be respected without continually justifying your existence.

Surround Yourself with Supportive People: Having healthy relationships is essential for rebuilding your confidence. Seek friends, relatives, or support groups who value and respect you for who you are. Positive connections can counteract the Negative feelings you may have absorbed from a narcissistic relationship, demonstrating that love and respect do not necessitate compromise or self-betrayal.

Practice assertiveness: Assertiveness allows you to properly explain your requirements and boundaries, which boosts your self-esteem. Learning to say "no" without feeling guilty or the need to justify yourself is liberating. When you assert yourself, you are saying that your voice, feelings, and desires are valuable.

Develop Internal Validation Habits: Establish routines or habits that allow you to routinely check in with yourself, such as writing, meditation, or self-reflective exercises. Consider asking yourself questions such as "How do I feel about this?" or "What do I want in this situation?" Tuning into your own voice strengthens your ability to value and trust yourself Your instincts trump external approval.

Separating self-worth from validation is a significant step in reclaiming your identity. By developing inner validation, identifying your unique skills, and setting boundaries, you can start to build a strong foundation of confidence. This newfound strength allows you to make decisions that follow your ideals and reaffirm your sense in your own worth, regardless of whether others approve or disapprove.

Reclaiming confidence and disconnecting your self-worth from external validation is a process of self-discovery. As you develop inner strength and change your self-perception, you empower yourself to live truly, free of narcissistic control. This increased confidence will guide you as you live a life full of respect, self-compassion, and resilience.

5. **Setting Strong, Healthy Boundaries**

- Learning to Say No: Establishing Limits

- Guarding Your Energy: Practical Steps for Self-Protection

- Communication Strategies: Asserting Your Needs without Guilt

Setting Strong and Healthy Boundaries

Establishing boundaries is critical for protecting yourself from the effects of narcissistic behavior and avoiding future harm. Boundaries protect your mental, emotional, and physical well-being by serving as a barrier against individuals who may drain or undermine you. Reclaiming your confidence frequently entails learning to say no, conserving your energy, and conveying your demands assertively and without shame. This chapter outlines a framework for setting boundaries that will enable you to protect your sense of self and live genuinely.

Learning to Say No: Setting Limits. Saying "no" is a powerful and vital skill, especially for people who have come out of situations where they have been encouraged to put others' demands before their own. In a narcissistic relationship, the tendency to Please others often leads to the erosion of one's own limits. To reclaim power, you must learn to say no effectively and unapologetically.

Understand Your Right to Say No: Saying no is not a selfish act; rather, it demonstrates self-respect. Recognizing your right to set boundaries helps to alleviate any guilt or hesitation you may feel. Every time you say no to anything that does not benefit you, you are saying yes to your own well-being and happiness.

Define your limits. Clearly: Think about what makes you uncomfortable or drains your energy. Identify non-negotiables, such as uninterrupted time for self-care, respectful communication, or emotional boundaries. Clearly outlining these boundaries enables you to successfully explain them when situations arise.

Use Direct, Concise Language: When setting limitations, keep The language clear. A simple "No, I'm unable to do that" or "That doesn't work for me" can be effective. Avoid over-explaining or justifying your decisions, since this may result in resistance from others who do not respect your boundaries.

Practice Self-Compassion: It may be unpleasant at first to reject requests that do not correspond with your values or well-being. Remind yourself that respecting your boundaries is a kind of self-care and an essential component of living truthfully. Every time you maintain a boundary, you demonstrate your dedication to self-respect.

Protecting Your Energy: Practical Steps for Self-Defense

Once you've established your limits, protecting your energy becomes a continuous discipline. Narcissistic people frequently consume other people's energy, leaving their prey feeling drained. Learning how to protect your energy might help you keep Balance and clarity.

Limit Interactions with Draining People: When feasible, spend less time with people who make you feel drained or uncomfortable. If you have to interact with someone who does not respect your boundaries, create time limits or choose locations in which you feel more in control.

Practice Mindful Detachment: Emotionally detaching yourself from the actions or opinions of others might assist you avoid becoming involved in manipulative or poisonous interactions. For example, if a narcissistic individual criticizes or provokes you, remember that their actions reflect their problems, not yours. Staying neutral can help keep their hostility from impacting your self-esteem.

Prioritize self-care rituals. Maintaining your energy takes continuous self-care.

Create practices that improve your mental, emotional, and physical health, such as journaling, meditation, or exercising. These routines help you concentrate yourself, making it easier to reject the influence of negative people.

Create "Energy Checkpoints": Take periodic pauses throughout difficult conversations to examine your feelings. These "checkpoints" help you determine whether someone's behavior is trespassing on your boundaries or draining your energy. If you find your energy dwindling, quietly excuse yourself or take a few long breaths to refocus.

Use Visual Boundaries: When interactions are unavoidable, imagine a barrier separating you and the other person. This mental visualization can strengthen your sense of self-protection, helping you to keep an emotional distance even when physical limits are not available.

Guarding your energy allows you to be grounded and robust. It emphasizes the idea that your well-being is the main priority that you deserve healthy, reciprocal relationships.

Communication Strategies: Asserting Your Needs Without Guilt.

Effectively asserting your wants is a key component of healthy limits. Communicating demands, however, can elicit emotions of shame in those who have been conditioned to prioritize others. Learning assertive communication strategies allows you to convey your boundaries clearly and confidently.

Use "I" Statements: When declaring a boundary, framing it as "I need" or "I feel" emphasizes your needs rather than blaming or criticizing the other person. Like the following: "I need time to myself right now" / "I feel more comfortable when we talk respectfully." This strategy can help you reduce defensiveness while also making your message clear.

Practice Assertiveness in Low-Stakes Situations: If setting boundaries seems frightening, start small. Practice

Asserting yourself in ordinary settings, such as denying an unexpected invitation or requesting space while you're busy. As you become more at ease, your confidence will rise, and expressing your wants will feel natural.

Maintain firm and consistent boundaries: Narcissistic people may try to test your commitment or make you feel guilty. Maintaining consistency in your communication, especially when confronted with criticism, reaffirms that your limits are non-negotiable. Repeat your needs as needed in a polite but strong tone.

Release Guilt as a Condition for Setting Boundaries Guilt frequently emerges while you are restoring your autonomy. Remind yourself that prioritizing your needs is not only acceptable, but also essential for healthy partnerships. Maintaining this perspective might help alleviate the guilt associated with setting boundaries.

De-escalate Emotional Situations: Narcissists may When presented with boundaries, they react adversely by seeking to provoke or guilt you. Maintain a calm and dispassionate demeanor, avoiding superfluous explanations or justifications.

You could respond: "I understand that this is difficult for you, but this is what I need." This relieves tension while maintaining your boundary.

Recognize Manipulative Responses: Narcissists may respond to limits by guilt-tripping, becoming angry, or playing the victim. Learn to recognize these emotions for what they are:

attempts to control your response. Staying aware of these strategies will help you avoid internalizing their reactions as personal failings.

Asserting your wants without shame is a powerful ability that boosts your self-esteem. When you communicate your limits firmly, you regain control of your life and show yourself the respect you deserve. Creating and maintaining healthy limits forms a protective shell that helps you to nurture your well-being while also attracting relationships based on mutual respect and understanding.

Creating solid, healthy boundaries is transformative. It is a huge step in regaining your confidence, allowing you to communicate with others from a position of strength rather than vulnerability. Boundaries allow you to protect your energy, express your needs openly, and form partnerships that promote your growth and pleasure.

6. **Breaking Free from Trauma Bonds**

- Understanding Emotional Attachment to Toxic Relationships

- Steps to Letting Go and Moving On

Breaking Free of Trauma Bonds

Breaking free from trauma attachments is a critical step toward self-recovery and empowerment. Trauma bonding is a psychological and emotional relationship created as a result of repeated abuse, manipulation, and emotional highs and lows. These attachments frequently form in toxic relationships, where the abuser swings between warm or remorseful conduct and damaging actions, resulting in a strong attachment that is difficult to sever. This pattern might leave you feeling dependent on the person who brings you misery, locking you in a relationship that damages your well-being. Recognizing and breaking free from trauma attachments is critical to healing and regaining your sense of self.

Understanding the emotional attachment to toxic relationships.

Trauma bonds are complicated emotional attachments that differ greatly from healthy relationships. They are frequently created in relationships characterized by strong emotions, resulting in a commitment based on survival instincts rather than love or mutual respect. Here are the psychological mechanisms behind trauma attachments and why they are so strong:

The Cycle of Abuse and Reconciliation: In a trauma connection, the abusive partner alternates between caring or loving acts and hurting ones. This creates a loop in which you may experience enormous relief or delight when things are "good" and profound anxiety or fear during the abusive moments. This unpredictability might lead to a reliance on these few times of serenity, strengthening the attachment.

The Brain's Response to Reward and Fear: The cycle of reward and fear causes the release of stress hormones such as cortisol and adrenaline, followed by dopamine when circumstances improve. This combination can lead to a physiological addiction to the relationship, as the brain develops acclimated to the pattern and seeks out the "highs" that come after periods of sorrow.

Self-fault and Guilt: Narcissistic and toxic relationships frequently influence you into believing that you are to fault for the dispute, which fuels emotions of guilt and self-blame. This idea can lead you to believe that if you just "try harder," things would improve, retaining your interest in the relationship despite the harm.

Distorted Perception of Love and Loyalty: The profound emotional experiences of a trauma bond can cause misunderstanding, leading you to mistake emotional suffering for love or loyalty. This misunderstanding makes it harder to view the connection as toxic, as you may feel a feeling of obligation to stay and "fix" problems.

dread of Loneliness and Abandonment: Trauma ties can cause a dread of being alone or abandoned, making you feel as if you rely on the person to feel whole or secure. The abuser may fuel this dread by emphasizing that you "can't live without them," which can exacerbate the attachment.

Understanding these mechanisms is the first step towards breaking free. Recognizing that these relationships are not love but rather a conditioned emotional response to an unhealthy cycle will help you begin to break free from your attachment.

Steps for Letting Go and Moving On

Releasing a trauma link involves time, patience, and self-compassion. It entails recognizing and eliminating the attachment's influence on you, frequently through a combination of self-reflection, emotional release, and external support. Here are some essential measures to help you let go and move forward:

Recognize the Reality of the Relationship: Accepting the true nature of the poisonous relationship is critical. You may have believed that things would get better or that the other person would change. Recognizing that their behavior is unlikely to change and is hurtful can help you begin to withdraw emotionally. To gain a clear picture of the situation, consider behavioral patterns rather than words or promises.

Reclaim Your Self-Worth: Trauma bonding can lower your self-esteem, making you feel unworthy of healthy, respectful love. Begin to focus on your own value, reminding yourself that you deserve mutually beneficial partnerships Care and respect. Engage in activities and affirmations that boost confidence and self-esteem, emphasizing that your happiness is not dependent on the poisonous individual.

Create Physical and Emotional Distance: Healing requires physical and emotional distance from the source of trauma. If feasible, limit contact, avoid areas connected with the person, and keep communication to a minimum. Emotional distance might also entail reframing your thoughts when you begin to miss them, reminding yourself of why the relationship was unhealthy rather than idealizing the past.

Lean on Your Support System: Breaking free from a trauma bond can be isolating. Seek help from friends, relatives, or a therapist who knows the complexities of toxic relationships. Talking openly about your experiences validates your sentiments and creates a sense of accountability, assuring your continued commitment to moving forward.

Practice Self-Compassion and Forgiveness: Trauma ties can cause long-term regret and shame, leading you to wonder why you stayed or suffered mistreatment. It's crucial to realize that these ties are complex, and the other person's emotional grasp on you was strong. Forgive yourself for previous decisions, acknowledging that you did your best in a tough scenario.

Focus on Personal Growth and Rediscovery: Regaining confidence after breaking a trauma bond requires rediscovering yourself outside of the poisonous relationship. Spend time reconnecting with hobbies, interests, and passions that you may have put aside. Exploring personal goals and objectives helps move your emphasis from the past to a future where you Feel empowered and whole.

Seek Professional Help When Needed: Trauma connections can be deeply ingrained, making it difficult to break free, especially if the attachment is based on unresolved trauma from the past. Therapy, particularly modalities such as cognitive-behavioral therapy (CBT) and trauma-focused therapy, can help you develop effective coping techniques and regain emotional strength.

Celebrate Small Victories: Breaking away from a trauma bond is a significant accomplishment, but it usually occurs in small steps rather than a single sweeping moment. Celebrate every small step forward, whether it's going a day without communication, fighting the impulse to check on the individual, or having a happy moment. Recognize that each move represents progress toward restoring your autonomy.

Accept the Healing Process: Healing is not linear, and it's normal to have times of doubt or melancholy. Be patient with yourself and recognize that it is acceptable to grieve. Accepting the healing process allows you to move on gradually, letting go of the past and opening yourself up to healthier relationships and a more real existence.

Breaking free from trauma bonds involves both release and self-renewal. It is about realizing that the relationship was formed out of survival rather than love, and that letting go is not only feasible, but also vital for your well-being. Each step you take on this road builds your confidence, validates your self-worth, and gives you the ability to live a life free of toxic relationships.

Moving forward and releasing the chains of trauma connections allows you to recover and Tell your life story and declare your entitlement to partnerships that value and support you.

Part III: Healing and Moving Forward**

7. **The Grieving Process: Allowing Yourself to Heal**

   - Stages of Grief in Narcissistic Relationships

   - Acknowledging Loss and Releasing Past Pain

Healing and Moving Forward

The Grief Process: Allowing Yourself to Heal Healing from a relationship with a narcissist is a path that includes emotional processing, release, and progressive self-rebuilding. It entails acknowledging and processing grief—an often unexpected but crucial component of moving on. mourning the termination of a narcissistic relationship is unlike ordinary mourning processes due to the numerous levels of manipulation, loss of self, and betrayal involved. Recognizing these stages, allowing yourself to fully experience them, and releasing previous pain are all important steps toward true recovery.

Stages of Grief in Narcissistic Relationships

While everyone's bereavement journey is unique, those who leave toxic or narcissistic relationships frequently encounter distinct emotional stages. Understanding these steps can help to normalize the process and lay the groundwork for future action.

Denial and Confusion.

The initial stage after leaving a narcissistic relationship is frequently characterized by a combination of denial and perplexity. During this stage, you may wonder if the relationship was genuinely as bad as it appeared, or you may rethink your decision to end it. This cognitive dissonance develops because narcissists frequently utilize manipulation tactics, such as gaslighting or love-bombing, that drive you to question reality. Denial is a protective strategy that allows you to gradually accept reality without experiencing extreme discomfort. Embrace this stage with patience, as it is a natural reaction to the breakdown of a deceptive relationship.

Anger and resentment

As denial fades, fury rises. This stage permits you to confront the injustices you experienced and feel betrayal, frustration, and express their pain openly. You may be angry at the narcissistic individual, yourself, or even those who enabled the conduct. Anger, when processed properly, is a sign of healing; it can fuel your determination to avoid similar circumstances in the future and establish tougher boundaries. Instead of repressing or allowing your anger to overtake you, channel it into positive behaviors like journaling, physical activities, or creative outlets.

Bargaining and "What-If" scenarios.

Bargaining is a stage where you could find yourself thinking about "what-if" scenarios. You may ponder if altering something about yourself or acting differently may have avoided the anguish. This stage displays a strong attachment to the relationship and a desire to restore control. It is crucial to remember that no amount of self-sacrifice, therapist, as voicing these emotions can help relieve discomfort.

Acceptance and Reclamation of the Self

Acceptance does not imply that you erase the memories of the relationship, but rather that you recognize it as a part of your past without allowing it to define you. Acceptance enables you to see the lessons learnt and acknowledge the strength you received from surviving the event. This stage is about incorporating your past experiences into your life story without allowing them to overpower your future. Acceptance provides a sense of liberty as you reclaim your autonomy, find your hobbies, and open yourself up to new, better relationships.

Acknowledging Loss and releasing Past Pain

Recognizing the loss of a narcissistic relationship entails confronting multiple layers of hurt, confusion, and broken expectations This process can be challenging since narcissistic relationships frequently blur boundaries and distorted self-perception. Here are important ways for releasing previous grief and making space for healing:

Allow Yourself to Feel: Releasing previous suffering demands accepting every emotion that occurs without judgment. Suppressing emotions merely prolongs grief, whereas expressing and acknowledging them hastens healing. Allow yourself to mourn, vent, or think on what was lost. Understand that experiencing pain is a normal part of the healing process and does not imply that you are not progressing.

Reframe Your Experience: Narcissistic interactions can distort your self-esteem and create negative views. Reframing your experience entails separating your self-worth from the negative signals you internalized throughout the relationship. Practice self-compassion by reminding yourself that the pain is not a reflection. It is the outcome of someone else's dysfunction, not your own worth. Shift your perspective from "I failed" to "I survived," and your experience will become a tribute to your perseverance.

Release Guilt and Self-Blame: Narcissists are skilled at making people feel accountable for their behavior, so those recovering from toxic relationships frequently experience guilt and self-blame. Recognize that you were dealing with an individual who thrived on control and manipulation. Practice self-forgiveness and remind yourself that your decisions were based on the knowledge and resources available at the time. Liberating yourself from guilt allows you to embrace the freedom to live your life truthfully.

Rituals for Closure: Rituals can provide symbolic closure, allowing you to shed the emotional hold of the past. You might consider Writing a letter expressing your emotions and then discarding it is a kind of letting go.

Other rituals, such as keeping a "healing journal" or practicing meditation and visualization, can act as emotional anchors, bringing solace while you process your loss. These rituals strengthen your commitment to moving forward and provide a physical means to mark the end of that chapter.

Engage in Self-Care and Self-Reclamation: Healing is more than just emotional processing; it is also about actively caring for your physical, mental, and spiritual well-being. Include activities that nourish you, such as exercise, creative outlets, nature walks, or hobbies that you enjoy. Self-care reminds you of your worth and allows you to rebuild a relationship with yourself, regardless of the trauma you've suffered.

Cultivate New ties: One of the most effective methods to release previous sorrow is to make new, supportive ties. Healthy relationships assist to replace bad patterns from the past with pleasant ones that reaffirm your value. While this may feel difficult at first, genuine friendships and connections will provide you with a fresh sense of trust, allowing you to see the world through a lens of safety rather than dread.

Embrace the Growth: As tough as it may appear, surviving a toxic relationship can lead to enormous personal growth. The path drives you to discover your own strength, define your ideals, and determine what you deserve. Reflecting on these growth periods allows you to see the experience as something that, while painful, eventually contributed. Congratulations on your resilience and self-awareness.

Embracing progress boosts your confidence and makes you feel empowered rather than victimized.

Look Forward with Purpose: Finally, focus on creating a future in which you may prosper on your terms. Setting new objectives and pursuing passions is an effective remedy to prior suffering because it redirects your focus away from the relationship and onto what you want for yourself. By crafting a vision for your future, you may start to rewrite your life story, replacing the old one with one of empowerment, self-compassion, and fulfillment.

The Value of Time and Patience

Healing from a narcissistic relationship takes time, tolerance, and dedication to self-compassion. Progress may seem slow at times, but each stride forward represents progress toward freedom and peace. Understand that Healing is non-linear, and setbacks are normal. The idea is to integrate the past so that you can move forward with clarity and strength.

Allowing yourself to properly grieve, releasing previous grief, and enjoying your journey helps you gradually break free from the narcissistic relationship. This process allows you to rediscover your sense of self, form new, meaningful connections, and create a future based on self-respect and empowerment.

8.   **Reclaiming Your Identity**

- Rebuilding Self-Worth: Practices for Self-Love

- Rediscovering Passions and Purpose

Reclaiming Your Identity.

Re-discovering your identity is one of the most empowering aspects of rehabilitation after leaving a bad relationship. Narcissistic relationships frequently distort your sense of self, destroying self-esteem, making you feel reliant, and separating you from who you truly are. Reclaiming your identity is an act of self-liberation that allows you to rebuild your self-esteem, find your passions, and live a life that reflects your true wants and beliefs.

Rebuilding Self-Worth: Practices for Self-Love When healing from narcissistic relationships, it is critical to rebuild one's self-esteem. Narcissists frequently undermine their partners' trust by questioning their choices, disregarding their needs, and distorting their perceptions of reality. This can make you feel unworthy and question your capacity to make sound decisions. Rebuilding self-worth involves counteracting Active self-compassion and affirmations of your intrinsic value can help to mitigate this damage.

Affirmations & Positive Self-Talk: Positive affirmations can help you rebuild your self-worth. It may appear simple, but speaking lovingly to oneself on a regular basis helps to modify your internal narrative. Use affirmations like "I am worthy of love and respect," "My needs are valid," and "I trust my instincts." Repeating these on a regular basis creates a more positive self-image, making it simpler to believe in yourself over time.

Reassess Core Beliefs: Narcissists frequently project their vulnerabilities, causing you to internalize their judgments. Begin by confronting any persistent thoughts that make you feel unworthy or inadequate. Write them down and challenge their veracity.

Replacing limiting ideas with empowering ones allows you to restore your sense of inner strength and eliminates the traces of their negativity.

Invest in Self-Care: Prioritizing self-care is a concrete approach to demonstrate that you deserve wonderful things. Physical activities, hobbies, and time spent in stimulating locations are all examples of self-care. Each act of self-care reaffirms your self-worth and rejects the internalized message that your needs are secondary.

Surround Yourself with Positive Influences: Seek out relationships with individuals that encourage and support you, which will assist to reaffirm your sense of value. Healthy friendships and community connections act as mirrors that highlight your best attributes, promoting growth and self-confidence. Self-esteem restoration occurs more quickly when it is nurtured in a positive, affirming social setting.

Rediscovering Passion and Purpose.

One of the most fundamental aspects of recovering your identity is about reconnecting with your hobbies and purpose. Narcissists frequently require constant attention, making it difficult for partners to pursue their own interests or hobbies. Rediscovering them can be an exciting part of the healing process, as you reconnect with the qualities of yourself that formerly made you happy.

Explore Forgotten Interests: Think about the things you previously loved but gave up during your partnership.

Whether it's a hobby, a professional interest, or a form of creative expression, reconnecting with these aspects of yourself can help reconstruct your identity. Make time to revisit these activities, even if only for a brief time each week.

Set Small, Achievable Goals: Start by establishing small, attainable goals relating to activities you enjoy. This could be learning something new, acquiring a talent, or Setting aside time to do something creative. Small goals not only bring joy, but they also generate momentum for a more fulfilling, purposeful existence.

Create a Vision for the Future: Moving beyond survival mode entails developing a meaningful vision for yourself. Outline a life that interests you, concentrating on personal and professional goals, relationships, and experiences that represent your personality. Defining a purpose or a set of goals provides a sense of direction and boosts your confidence in pursuing what is actually important to you.

Engage in Self-Reflection: Check in with yourself on a regular basis to see what makes you happy and fulfilled. Reclaiming your identity entails continuous self-discovery, rather than conforming to someone else's expectations. Accept the adventure of getting there Understand yourself better, and be open to how your hobbies and passions may change as you grow.

Reclaiming your identity after a narcissistic relationship is liberating and necessary for going forward. This path is about more than just recovering from a relationship; it's also about finding your sense of purpose, confidence, and joy. Each step you take to improve your self-esteem and embrace your passions is a step toward a future founded on genuine self-acceptance and joy.

9. **Embracing Forgiveness and Self-Compassion**

- Forgiving Yourself, Not the Narcissist

- Healing through Kindness: Practicing Self-Compassion Daily

Embracing forgiveness and self-compassion.

Learning to forgive yourself, rather than the narcissist, is one of the most difficult but necessary steps in recovering from a narcissistic relationship. Narcissistic relationships frequently leave survivors with feelings of self-blame, guilt, and regret. Learning to forgive yourself and practice self-compassion allows you to go forward with a lighter emotional weight while healing and recovering your self-worth.

Forgive Yourself, Not The Narcissist.

The concept of forgiveness in the context of a toxic relationship is complex. Many survivors are expected to forgive the narcissist, but this might feel impossible and improper, especially when there has been intentional harm and deception. Instead, focus on forgiving yourself. Narcissists are extremely adept at lying, gaslighting, and emotional manipulation They frequently leave their spouses questioning their own conduct and self-worth. Recognize that you tried your best in a very difficult situation, and that the narcissist's conduct does not represent your value.

Letting Go of Regret: You may regret remaining in the relationship or failing to recognize the warning flags sooner. Forgiving yourself entails acknowledging that leaving a toxic relationship is difficult, especially when manipulation is present. Remind yourself that you were under emotional coercion and control, which is meant to be disorienting. Remove the burden of regret by acknowledging that leaving a narcissistic relationship involves enormous courage, and each step you've taken demonstrates your strength.

Accepting Your Vulnerability: Many people are embarrassed about being exposed to the strategies used by a narcissist. However, this susceptibility is frequently caused by characteristics like empathy, generosity, and trust—all of which are strengths rather than faults. Recognize that these attributes indicate your potential for compassion and connection, and let go of any shame that comes with them.

Releasing Self-Blame: Narcissists frequently implant self-blame in their spouses, making them feel accountable for the narcissist's behavior. Recognize that their actions are motivated by their own unsolved issues and personality traits. As you let go of the false guilt they may have imposed on you, you restore your inner power. This change enables you to free yourself from the narcissist's influence and see that their behavior was never a reflection of your worth.

Viewing Yourself with Compassion: Consider what you would say to a friend in your position. Frequently, we hold ourselves to standards that we would never place on others. Remind yourself that you are worthy of the same empathy you show others, and give yourself permission to recover without judgment.

Healing with Kindness: Daily Practice of Self-Compassion

Self-compassion is the cornerstone of recovery from a narcissistic relationship. Narcissistic manipulation frequently results in severe self-criticism, as survivors may grow to believe they are inadequate or imperfect. Self-compassion helps to counteract this negative self-narrative by fostering gentle, understanding self-talk and a renewed regard for oneself.

Engage in self-soothing practices. Self-compassion entails caring for oneself at times of sorrow or struggle, just as one would comfort a loved one. Practicing self-soothing can be as easy as saying pleasant words to a friend in your position. Frequently, we hold ourselves to standards that we would never place on others. Remind yourself that you are worthy of the same empathy you show others, and give yourself permission to recover without judgment.

Self-forgiveness is essential for overcoming the long-term repercussions of a narcissistic relationship. By abandoning self-blame and cultivating compassion, you pave the way for deeper, more meaningful recovery. This inner kindness enables you to move forward with a renewed sense of self-worth, free of the shame and guilt instilled by others. Embracing forgiveness and self-compassion is not only liberating, but also essential for recovering a joyous, meaningful life that is entirely yours.

Part IV: Thriving Beyond Toxic Relationships**

10. **Building Resilience for a Narcissist-Free Life**

- How to Recognize and Avoid Toxic Relationships

- Maintaining Your Boundaries and Self-Respect in New Relationships

Building Resilience for a Narcissist-Free Life.

Leaving a toxic relationship with a narcissist is a huge accomplishment, but genuine healing is learning how to live and build resilience in a life free of manipulative behaviors. This resilience enables you to see possible red flags, maintain your boundaries, and develop healthy, caring relationships in the future. Building a narcissist-free life necessitates self-awareness, boundary maintenance, and a dedication to personal development. Here, we look at strategies to prevent sliding back into toxic patterns while maintaining the self-esteem and confidence required to succeed.

How To Identify and Avoid Toxic Relationships

After being in a relationship with a narcissist, you're probably more aware of certain actions that indicate manipulation or toxicity. However, identifying and avoiding toxic interactions can still be difficult, especially when some people may appear to be charming or well-meaning at first. Building resilience begins with recognizing these warning flags and putting your emotional well-being first.

Identifying Early Red Flags: Many narcissists and toxic people demonstrate certain behaviors early in their relationships, even if slightly. Keep an eye out for behaviors such as excessive self-focus, a need for constant adoration, an unwillingness to accept responsibility, or disregard for your limits. These characteristics may not always be visible, but by being aware of them, you can prevent becoming involved in another bad relationship.

Listen to Your Gut Instinct: Your instincts often detect small clues about a person's conduct before your mind does. If you feel uneasy, exhausted, or wary around someone without a clear Consider it a potential sign that something isn't right. Trusting oneself is crucial for avoiding future toxic relationships and protecting your emotional well-being.

Questioning Rapid Relationship Progression: Narcissists and toxic people frequently hurry through the early phases of relationships to maintain control before their conduct becomes obvious. If someone presses for intimate closeness or commitment too fast, it can be a warning sign. Taking things slowly gives you time to analyze their genuine character before becoming emotionally attached.

Observing How They Treat Others: Pay attention to how a potential spouse or friend interacts with those around them, particularly those in service positions, as well as their family and friends. Toxic persons may exhibit dismissive or haughty conduct towards others, which When the initial appeal wears off, it generally foreshadows how they will treat you later.

Aligning Values and Goals: A lack of shared values and life goals can cause problems in any relationship, but toxic relationships frequently escalate into control concerns. Determine whether a new individual respects your values and ambitions, as a mismatch may indicate a potential conflict for autonomy.

Maintaining Boundaries and Self-Respect in New Relationships

One of the most important abilities for living outside of toxic relationships is the ability to set and maintain boundaries. Boundaries are crucial in any relationship, but they are especially important for someone healing from a narcissistic relationship, which generally erodes self-esteem and undermines personal limitations.

Strengthening your boundaries enhances your resilience and self-worth, giving you the power to Develop future relationships on your own terms.

Setting boundaries begins with clarity. Determine your non-negotiables, values, and what makes you feel comfortable and valued. Establishing and adhering to your standards provides a solid foundation for your autonomy and confidence. Clearly defined boundaries keep you safe from manipulation and help you realize when someone's behavior exceeds the line.

Assertive Communication: Effectively communicating your limits is critical for ensuring that they are respected. To explain your wants without seeming accusatory, use "I" words like "I need time for myself" or "I'm uncomfortable when…". Being aggressive and unambiguous demonstrates respect for oneself and allows others to understand where you stand. Assertive communication is also a powerful Signal to others that you care about your own well-being.

Recognize When to Enforce Boundaries: In toxic relationships, boundaries are frequently ignored or abused. However, in healthy relationships, boundaries are recognized and valued. Be prepared to enforce your boundaries by taking action if someone consistently disregards them. This could entail restricting contact, imposing a consequence, or, in extreme situations, terminating the relationship. Setting limits reinforces self-esteem and assists you in avoiding compromising circumstances.

Self-respect is fundamentally linked to self-care. Regular self-care reminds you that you are worthy of compassion and respect, and it strengthens your commitment to your own well-being. Whether through interests, connections, or alone time, self-care offers you the strength to maintain your boundaries and resist pressure to compromise.

Accepting Healthy Conflicts: Healthy relationships may include conflicts, but they respect boundaries and avoid manipulation. Learning to negotiate conflict in a healthy way, via open communication and mutual respect, strengthens your resilience. A narcissist-free life is not without conflict, but it is free of harmful, boundary-breaking conduct.

Building a Strong Support Network: Spending time with helpful people boosts your self-esteem and reminds you of what good, respectful relationships look like. Family, friends, or a support group can offer encouragement and accountability as you develop resilience. A robust support network makes you less inclined to endure toxicity because you know you're not alone.

Regular Self-Reflection: Building resilience requires constant self-reflection. Regularly check whether your needs are met and whether your limits are respected in new relationships. This keeps you aware of any patterns that may emerge and gives you the ability to address problems early on.

Recognize and celebrate every step you take towards living a narcissist-free existence. Every time you set boundaries, state your demands, or select a good connection over a poisonous one, you strengthen your resilience. Celebrating your progress fosters a positive self-image and prepares you for continued success.

By cultivating resilience, you lay the groundwork for a fulfilling, narcissist-free life. Recognizing toxic behavior, setting boundaries, and cultivating your self-esteem will enable you to thrive beyond the shadows of previous relationships. This resilience not only serves as a safeguard against potential future injury, but it also affirms Your development, strength, and dedication to living a life that reflects who you truly are.

11. **Finding Support and Moving Forward**

- Reaching Out: The Role of Friends, Family, and Support Groups

- Living Authentically: How to Thrive as Your True Self

Finding Support and Moving Forward

Healing from a relationship with a narcissist can be isolating, but seeking support is critical to establishing a healthier, more resilient life. This journey requires developing connections that empower, support, and uplift you while recovering your identity and the delight of being completely yourself. Cultivating a supporting network of friends, family, and even support groups allows you to stay anchored in healthy relationships while also giving you the strength to thrive as yourself.

Friends, family, and support groups play a crucial role in reaching out.

Building a Support Network: One of the most important stages towards long-term rehabilitation is to surround yourself with people who sincerely care about your well-being. Trusted friends and family offer emotional and practical assistance, serving as sounding boards for your experiences and reinforcing your value. These interactions remind you of your importance outside of toxic situations, laying the groundwork for resilience.

Embracing Vulnerability with Trusted People: After witnessing manipulation, it's natural to be afraid to trust others again. However, sharing your story with people who are caring and nonjudgmental can be really empowering. Allowing yourself to be vulnerable with the proper people might help you overcome lingering self-doubt and practice healthy communication and trust.

Seeking Professional and Peer Support: Participating in a support group or connecting with people who have shared similar situations can be transformative. In these settings, you can find validation from people who understand the consequences of narcissistic abuse. Sharing coping skills, listening to others' stories, Celebrating progress together provides therapeutic insights that help you move ahead.

Therapy as a Safe Haven: Therapy can be a very helpful tool in the healing process. Trained specialists provide an unbiased perspective, assisting you in overcoming trauma and reconnecting with your inner self. Therapists can help you unravel the remaining effects of narcissistic influence and develop resilience techniques for long-term healing.

Live Authentically: How to Thrive as Your True Self

Rediscovering What Matters: Surviving past toxic relationships entails reconnecting with what truly makes you happy. Pursue your hobbies, make personal goals, and allow yourself to dream again. Reclaiming your passions and desires can help restore your sense of self, which may have been distorted by narcissistic influences.

Setting Intentional Goals: To live truly, define your Set your own goals and priorities without regard for other influences. Consider what success and happiness look like for you, and set meaningful goals that represent your values and desires. Setting objectives based on self-discovery empowers you to live a purposeful and fulfilling life.

Practicing Self-Compassion: Accepting your genuine self entails letting go of perfectionism and learning to treat yourself with care. This includes forgiving yourself for past mistakes, embracing your flaws, and enjoying your accomplishments, no matter how minor. Self-compassion increases resilience and reminds you that you are deserving of love and respect just the way you are.

Creating Joyful Connections: Moving forward, good partnerships must prioritize mutual respect, trust, and understanding. Choose connections that celebrate your growth and respect your limits, while departing Follow those that drain or detract from your well-being. Genuine connections enable you to feel joy, love, and support in a way that feeds your spirit.

Embracing Your Journey: Healing and thriving are continuous processes that necessitate patience and self-care. Recognize and celebrate each step forward as a demonstration of your strength and resilience. Accept the trip as a continuing road of progress, allowing your genuine self to shine through in ways that a toxic relationship previously masked.

By choosing to thrive, you claim a future free of previous hurt, where you can live with purpose, self-esteem, and joy. With the help of people who truly care, you lay the groundwork for a life that celebrates the essence of who you are and opens doors to meaningful, loving partnerships. Thriving after a toxic relationship is more than simply surviving; it is about reclaiming and appreciating the life you deserve.

12. **Empowered for Good: Embracing Your Future with Confidence**

- Final Reflections on Freedom and Growth

- Continuing Your Journey of Self-Discovery and Inner Peace

Empowered for Good: Embracing Your Future With Confidence

Leaving a toxic relationship with a narcissist is a life-changing adventure that will leave you smarter, more resilient, and deeply aware of your own value. As you go, the voyage of self-discovery and growth continues, allowing you to live your life with renewed confidence and purpose. Embracing this new chapter entails carrying on the lessons learnt, continuing on the path to inner peace, and feeling empowered to live a life that genuinely reflects who you are.

Final Thoughts on Freedom and Growth

Getting out of a bad relationship feels like a breath of fresh air after years of confinement. Beyond the first comfort, there is an even greater reward—the gift of a life lived on your Own terminology. This newfound independence allows you to reflect on how you've developed and realize that, with your strength and perseverance, you've not only survived but flourished.

Recognizing Your Strength: One of the most effective components of recovery is realizing how strong you are. You've faced deception, emotional turmoil, and the difficulties of quitting a toxic relationship. Embracing your resilience allows you to move forward with confidence, knowing that you are capable of navigating any situation that may arise.

Redefining Your beliefs: Leaving a relationship with a narcissist can help you gain a better knowledge of your own beliefs and non-negotiables. Reflecting on your experiences allows you to prioritize values such as respect, trust, empathy, and mutual support.

These values presently serve as guiding principles for future partnerships throughout your life.

Accepting Boundaries as Acts of Self-Love: The limits you've learned to establish and enforce are more than just defensive measures; they're acts of self-love. Maintaining these boundaries affirms your own worth and respects your demands. The newfound ability to say "no" or "this doesn't feel right" is a powerful type of self-respect that will benefit you in all aspects of life.

Letting Go of Perfection: Narcissistic relationships frequently impose false expectations and perfectionism. You can now let go of these pressures and adopt an attitude that accepts flaws. You are valuable just the way you are, and your worth does not depend on satisfying someone else's unrealistic expectations. Freedom is in This sense is the ability to be completely and genuinely yourself.

Continue Your Journey of Self-Discovery and Inner Peace.

The end of a destructive relationship signaled the start of a lifelong journey of self-discovery. As you begin this new chapter, continue to endeavor to understand yourself, your needs, and your passions, while fostering inner peace through practices that promote resilience and joy.

Commitment to Growth: Healing and personal development are lifelong tasks. Accept every step of the path, knowing that each trial and accomplishment contributes to your wisdom and strength. Growth entails constantly learning, adjusting, and honoring your genuine self. Being open to change enables you to approach new experiences with curiosity and resilience.

Rediscovering Joy and Purpose is one of the most lovely benefits of healing and rediscovering delight. You now have the freedom to pursue previously unfulfilled hobbies and goals. Allowing joy into your life, whether through a pastime, a new employment, or simply appreciating the peace and quiet of isolation, gets you closer to inner serenity and fulfillment.

Practicing   Self-Compassion: Forgiving yourself and being gentle to yourself are critical components of healing. Self-compassion reminds you that you are not defined by your history or the sorrow you have endured. You are allowed to make errors, heal at your own time, and prioritize your own happiness. Self-compassion helps you approach each day with tolerance and understanding.

Building a Community of Support and Positivity: Thriving involves interacting with others who uplift, inspire, and I respect you. Surround yourself with people that encourage your development and respect your boundaries. A robust support system strengthens your sense of self and provides the framework for living authentically without fear of judgment or criticism.

Trusting Yourself and Moving Forward With Confidence: Reclaiming your intuition is one of the most empowering aspects of the journey. Trusting yourself and your decisions is an important step in building a fulfilling future. You've learned to spot manipulation and control, and you can now confidently pick positive relationships, surroundings, and experiences in your life.

Finding Inner Peace: Finally, finding peace is an essential component of thriving. Inner serenity is not the absence of obstacles, but rather the presence of acceptance and balance.

Practices such as mindfulness, meditation, and journaling, Simply spending time in nature can center you and help you stay connected to yourself in a meaningful way.

Moving forward, each moment presents an opportunity to live authentically and confidently, rooted on your newfound resilience. You have the freedom to be yourself, to live the life you deserve, and to welcome each day with an open heart. Embracing your future entails acknowledging the path that led you here and appreciating the strength that will propel you ahead into a life of genuine joy and fulfillment.

Conclusion**

- The Path to Lasting Peace: A Life Beyond Narcissistic Influence

The Path to Lasting Peace: Living Beyond Narcissistic Influence

Reaching the finish of this trip represents amazing courage, progress, and resilience. Breaking free from narcissistic influence has taken you through multiple stages of self-discovery, healing, and empowerment. You've learned about the complexities of narcissism, how it distorted your self-worth, and how to regain your confidence via active self-respect and boundary establishing. The route forward now offers you to embrace a life of permanent peace—one defined by the brightness of your actual, resilient self, rather than the shadows of former relationships.

Living with Inner Peace.

Inner serenity is something you offer yourself. It's the unwavering serenity that comes from understanding your worth and having the courage to defend it. Living with inner peace is cultivating a feeling of balance in which problems no longer upset your confidence and destructive actions from others do not undermine your self-esteem. This type of serenity necessitates accepting the healing path as a continuing process, allowing you to completely realize your potential while letting go of any leftover guilt, self-blame, or self-doubt.

Letting Go of Past Pain: As you heal, you've most likely felt the weight of old pains caused by narcissistic relationships. To achieve long-term tranquility, it is critical to let go of these painful memories. This does not imply ignoring or dismissing your past experiences, but rather deciding not to let them govern your current. It's about confirming that the chapter of narcissistic influence has ended and that you're empowered to write the future chapters on your own terms.

Celebrating Your perseverance: The capacity to recognize and leave a harmful relationship demonstrates tremendous perseverance. Every step you've taken, from detecting narcissistic traits to establishing solid boundaries, has provided you with vital tools for future struggles. Celebrate this strength since it serves as the foundation for long-term harmony.

Committing to Self-Care: To achieve long-term tranquility, you must commit to taking care of yourself on a daily basis. Make time in your life for activities and practices that nourish your spirit, such as mindfulness, exercise, and creative expression. Self-care strengthens your mental, emotional, and physical well-being while reminding you that you are worthy of attention, kindness, and respect.

Embracing Forgiveness: One of the last steps of healing is embracing forgiveness. This does not imply absolving the narcissist of their actions; rather, it entails forgiving yourself for the time you spent in the relationship and any self-doubt you may have developed. Forgiving yourself allows you to release the burden of regret and go on guilt-free. It confirms that you are whole and worthy of peace.

Developing a New Vision for Your Future

As you progress, developing a vision for the future becomes an inspiring trip in its own right. Imagine a life filled with people who respect your limits, encourage your development, and appreciate you for who you truly are. Building this new vision requires pursuing objectives, passions, and relationships that reflect your genuine self, free of the concerns and constraints of previous destructive relationships influences.

Embracing Purposeful Connections:
The relationships in your new chapter

should reflect what you've learned. Surround yourself with people that really encourage, appreciate, and inspire you. Nurture ties based on mutual understanding and trust, as well as respect for boundaries. Purposeful interactions promote inner calm and help you to grow without jeopardizing your health.

Pursuing Joy and Fulfillment: A life free of narcissistic influence is an open canvas on which you can paint moments of joy, creativity, and fulfillment. Revisit hobbies, pursue new interests, or participate in activities that excite and energize you. Each joyful pastime you engage in demonstrates your resilience and provides a benefit to your well-being.

Embodying Confidence and Self-Respect: Knowing and accepting your own worth is essential for long-term peace. Moving forward, This self-respect allows you to interact with the world with confidence. It enables you to set boundaries that protect your serenity, express your wants without feeling guilty, and make decisions that emphasize your satisfaction. Living with self-respect is an expression of your dedication to yourself and your well-being.

Continue the journey of self-discovery.

Your healing journey doesn't end here; rather, it is a continuous process that encourages you to explore new sides of yourself. Allow yourself to grow and progress by welcoming events that deepen your character and resilience. Continue to pursue self-discovery since it is through this exploration that you will be able to establish a life of calm, meaning, and happiness.

Setting New Goals: Spend time imagining what you want for yourself in this new chapter. Setting goals for the future, whether they are for personal development, career advancement, or relationships, gives you a sense of purpose and direction. Aligning your activities with your real desires strengthens your commitment to a fulfilling life.

Practicing Gratitude: Recognizing your benefits on a regular basis will help you feel more at ease inside. Gratitude directs your attention to what is positive, allowing you to create contentment and remain grounded. Practicing thankfulness also validates your journey by acknowledging the insight, strength, and growth acquired from leaving abusive relationships.

Embracing Compassion and Kindness: As you heal, choose to be compassionate to yourself and others.

Compassion, both self-directed and outward, keeps your heart open and strong. Living with compassion improves your ability to connect with others in meaningful ways, encouraging a tranquil, balanced, and rewarding lifestyle.

Final Thoughts on Lasting Peace

Reaching long-term tranquility after a narcissistic relationship is a significant accomplishment. It represents that you have not only survived, but also transcended the agony, enjoying a life of self-respect, authenticity, and inner peace. This voyage demonstrates your strength, resilience, and capacity for growth.

You are now empowered to move on, ready to embrace life with an open heart and a clear mind. By claiming your peace, you have liberated yourself from poisonous influences, allowing you to live with confidence and delight. You have the freedom to choose relationships that value you, pursue aspirations that inspire you, and follow a path that reflects your authentic, beautiful self. This is the way to long-term peace—a life free of narcissistic influences, full of self-love, purpose, and fulfillment.

www.ingramcontent.com/pod-product-compliance
Lightning Source LLC
Chambersburg PA
CBHW051047250726
48656CB00001B/180